ALEXIS ZEGERMAN

Theatre work includes *The Fever Syndrome* (Hampstead Theatre); *Holy Sh!t* (Kiln Theatre); *The Steingolds* (National Theatre Studio; finalist for the Susan Smith Blackburn Prize); *Lucky Seven* (Hampstead Theatre Pearson Writer in Residence); *Killing Brando* (Òran Mór, A Play, A Pie and A Pint season/ Paines Plough Theatre Company at the Young Vic); *I Ran the World* (Royal Court/Flight 5065); *Marriage and Noise* (Soho Theatre). Alexis is currently under commission with Hampstead Theatre and the Manhattan Theatre Club, New York.

Film work includes the screenplay *Arthur's Whiskey*, starring Diane Keaton and David Harewood.

Radio work includes the two comedy series *Mum's on the Run* and *School Runs*, and the radio plays *Déjà Vu* (Prix Europa Special Commendation), *Jump*, *The Singing Butler*, *Are You Sure?*, *Ronnie Gecko* (Richard Imison Award) and *Cold Tapes* (Spotify).

## Other Original Plays for Young People to Perform from Nick Hern Books

100 Christopher Heimann, Neil Monaghan, Diene Petterle

BANANA BOYS Evan Placey

BOYS Ella Hickson

BRAINSTORM Ned Glasier, Emily Lim and Company Three

BROKEN BISCUITS Tom Wells

BURYING YOUR BROTHER IN THE PAVEMENT Jack Thorne

THE CHANGING ROOM Chris Bush

CHAOS Laura Lomas

COCKROACH Sam Holcroft

COMMENT IS FREE James Fritz

THE DOMINO EFFECT AND OTHER PLAYS Fin Kennedy

THE FALL James Fritz

GIRLS LIKE THAT Evan Placey

IS MY MICROPHONE ON? Jordan Tannahill

THE IT Vivienne Franzmann

PRONOUN Evan Placey

SAME Deborah Bruce

THE SMALL HOURS Katherine Soper

START SWIMMING James Fritz

STUFF Tom Wells

THE TRIALS Dawn King

TUESDAY Alison Carr

THE URBAN GIRL'S GUIDE TO CAMPING AND OTHER PLAYS Fin Kennedy

THE WARDROBE Sam Holcroft

WHEN THEY GO LOW Natalie Mitchell

WHEN THIS IS OVER Ned Glasier, Sadeysa Greenaway-Bailey and Company Three

## Platform

Platform is a series of plays for young actors with all or mainly female casts, which put young women and their stories at the heart of the action – commissioned by Tonic Theatre, published and licensed by Nick Hern Books.

BRIGHT. YOUNG. THINGS. Georgia Christou

HEAVY WEATHER Lizzie Nunnery

THE GLOVE THIEF Beth Flintoff

THE LIGHT BURNS BLUE Silva Semerciyan

RED Somalia Seaton

SECOND PERSON NARRATIVE Jemma Kennedy

THIS CHANGES EVERYTHING Joel Horwood

For more information, visit www.tonictheatre-platform.co.uk

Alexis Zegerman

# SHOUT

NICK HERN BOOKS
London
www.nickhernbooks.co.uk

**A Nick Hern Book**

*Shout* first published in Great Britain in 2024 as a paperback original by Nick Hern Books Limited, The Glasshouse, 49a Goldhawk Road, London W12 8QP

*Shout* copyright © 2024 Alexis Zegerman

Alexis Zegerman has asserted her moral right to be identified as the author of this work

Cover image: iStock.com/FTiare

Designed and typeset by Nick Hern Books, London
Printed in the UK by Mimeo Ltd, Huntingdon, Cambridgeshire PE29 6XX

A CIP catalogue record for this book is available from the British Library

ISBN 978 1 83904 374 1

**CAUTION**  All rights whatsoever in this play are strictly reserved. Requests to reproduce the text in whole or in part should be addressed to the publisher.

**Amateur Performing Rights**  Applications for performance, including readings and excerpts, by amateurs in the English language throughout the world should be addressed to the Performing Rights Department, Nick Hern Books, The Glasshouse, 49a Goldhawk Road, London W12 8QP, *tel* +44 (0)20 8749 4953, *email* rights@nickhernbooks.co.uk, except as follows:

*Australia*: ORiGiN Theatrical, *email* enquiries@originmusic.com.au, *web* www.origintheatrical.com.au

*New Zealand*: Play Bureau, 20 Rua Street, Mangapapa, Gisborne, 4010, *tel* +64 21 258 3998, *email* info@playbureau.com

*United States and Canada*: Casarotto Ramsay and Associates Ltd, see details below

**Professional Performing Rights**  Applications for performance by professionals in any medium and in any language throughout the world (including by amateur stock companies in the USA and Canada) should be addressed to Casarotto Ramsay and Associates Ltd, *email* rights@casarotto.co.uk, www.casarotto.co.uk

No performance of any kind may be given unless a licence has been obtained. Applications should be made before rehearsals begin. Publication of this play does not necessarily indicate its availability for amateur performance.

www.nickhernbooks.co.uk/environmental-policy

*Shout* was commissioned as part of the 2024 National Theatre Connections Festival and premiered by youth theatres across the UK, including a performance at the National Theatre in June 2024.

Each year the National Theatre asks ten writers to create new plays to be performed by young theatre companies all over the country. From Scotland to Cornwall and Northern Ireland to Norfolk, Connections celebrates great new writing for the stage – and the energy, commitment and talent of young theatremakers.

www.nationaltheatre.org.uk/connections

**Author's Note**

Selective mutism is an anxiety disorder, present in at least one in every 140 children and teenagers. People suffering from selective mutism will not be able to speak in certain, or all environments, most commonly school. The disorder is under-diagnosed as it is often mistaken for other things, like being shy, depressed or difficult. It presents more commonly in girls than boys. Selective mutism is the current terminology used, but this may change over time.

You will know someone with selective mutism – even if you don't know it.

It is in the nature of the subject matter that the play is designed to be as inclusive as possible. There is ample opportunity for non-speaking roles, movement-only roles, supporting-artist roles.

Parts can be multi-roled. The characters in the Calming Room are funny, but please ensure we laugh with them and not at them – they're not to be ridiculed.

Dana is written as a girl.
Tristan is written as a boy.

All other parts can be played by any gender. If a company wishes for the characters of Dana and Tristan to be gender-swapped, or non-binary, this is entirely possible – please contact me via Nick Hern Books (see details on page 4) for any script changes necessary.

The song on pages 30–32 is a suggestion – feel free to change it, but the spirit and energy of what the song conveys in the script should be adhered to. (Other suggestions would be songs like 'good 4 u' by Olivia Rodrigo, 'So What' by P!nk, 'Experiment on Me' by Halsey or 'Misery Business' by Paramore.)

The script published here contains a few mild swear words. There are 'no swear' alternatives to these, available from Nick Hern Books, which can be swapped in.

The play is set in a school or sixth-form college. There are chairs all over the stage, which can be moved around to represent each scene's location.

Transitions between scenes are designed to be smooth and fluid.

Text messages or other digital media in the play are designed to be spoken aloud by another actor standing behind the actor who is texting, but feel free to let your imagination go.

This goes for all stage directions – they are open to your interpretation, as long as the story and characters' journeys are honoured.

Lastly, have the confidence and courage to lean into the silences in the play. Hold and embrace the uncomfortableness that can accompany silence.

*A.Z.*

*For Maya Angelou, Albert Einstein, Greta Thunberg, Lola,
and the millions of young people all over the world
who find it difficult to speak.*

*You are heard.*

**Characters**

DANA
TRISTAN
VIV
MAYA
TRINH
TRISTAN
TOM
SAM
NAV
YAZ
ADMISSIONS ADVISER
CLASSICS TEACHER
CON
JONO
ANITA
TONI
PETE
SAINI
HOLLY
MO
THERAPIST
HEADTEACHER
LAURA
LIBRARIAN

STUDENTS

**Note**

Words in [*square brackets*] are intention, not to be spoken.

*Silence.*

*Then –*

*The cast come on, chattering, talking, overlapping – certain conversations ping out. The chairs are set up like benches in a schoolyard.* DANA *walks through the people, weaves through the noise. Her backpack is heavy. She doesn't look like the hero of our story, or even her own story, but she is. She is silent.*

STUDENT 1. Word.

STUDENT 2. Word.

STUDENT 3. Word.

STUDENT 4. Yeah, I mean –

STUDENT 5. Then he said –

STUDENT 6. Unreal, bruv.

STUDENT 7. Then she said –

STUDENT 6. Oh, my days!

STUDENT 8. LOL.

STUDENT 5. A hundred and ten per cent.

STUDENT 1. What you doing after school?

STUDENT 2. Why didn't you answer my DM?

STUDENT 3. I'm airing you.

STUDENT 2. Talking to me is a funny way of airing me.

STUDENT 6. Rude.

STUDENT 1. Word.

DANA. Words.

*When* DANA *speaks, she is addressing the audience. This is her interior voice, and nobody onstage can hear her. Only us.*

Words are coming at you at a thousand miles a second. In the beginning was the word. A sound. A big bang. I speak, therefore I am. And if you're not the loudest voice –

*Everyone around her gets louder –*

STUDENT 4. A hundred and ten per cent is not a thing!

DANA (*tries to shout*). If you don't shout, and scream, and make your mark –

STUDENT 7. She said 'Girl, you have five seconds to get out of my face' –

DANA. Then how do you get heard?

STUDENT 5. What did she say?

STUDENT 7. She said, 'Suck my' –

STUDENT 6. Rude.

DANA. If you don't speak, do you even exist?

*Everyone is silent. Still. A light on* DANA.

If a tree falls in the forest, but no one hears it… Has it even fallen?

*Schoolyard. Everyone is milling in their cliques – doing their various things – TikTok; chatting, plaiting hair.* DANA *walks through, heading to the school building, head down.*

VIV, *her best friend, runs up to her.*

VIV. Hey, Dana.

DANA *smiles and waves.*

How are you?

DANA *nods – 'Okay.' She points to* VIV *– 'You?'*

I'm good. Apart from the imminent depletion of the tundra's permafrost.

And the oceans are absorbing the heat equivalent of five atomic bombs per second.

In the selfish, immediate short-term, I'm good.

Hey, I've been choreographing this really cool thing for our TikTok channel.

*She does a not very cool dance, but it is definitely committed. DANA really enjoys watching her – she gets into it a bit.*

Oh yeah. Oh yeah. Look at her go. Shut that front door.

*The COOL GIRLS stare at them goofing about.*

MAYA. Fr-eeeeeeeeak.

TRINH. Mute.

VIV. Just ignore them.

What time's your appointment with the admissions adviser?

*DANA holds up ten fingers.*

Ah, okay, mine's at eleven. I think I'm definitely going Leeds top choice, then Manchester, then Salford, then the rest are really, like, back-ups if I have a brain haemorrhage during the exam. Which might actually happen in English.

*She stops as TRISTAN, and a group of his friends, walk across the school recreation area, sports bags casually slung over shoulders like they're in* Britain's Next Top Model. TRISTAN *is holding a rugby ball. Everyone stops to stare at* TRISTAN.

TRISTAN. Go wide.

TOM. Don't smash it into my face.

SAM. His face is his fortune.

NAV. Which is why he's broke.

*TOM runs backwards to catch the rugby ball, and knocks into VIV. He ignores her. The COOL GIRLS laugh.*

VIV. Oops, sorry.

*DANA helps her up. VIV brushes herself off, still staring at TRISTAN.*

Hey, Tristan.

*He walks past her and over to the COOL GIRLS.*

MAYA (*to* TRISTAN). Careful, The Mute is staring at you.

TRINH. Do you think it's catching? Her cow-eye stare will turn you cold-stone mute.

YAZ. F-uh-reeeeeeak.

VIV (*shouts over*). Privileged douchebags! Instead of getting a car for your birthday, why don't you plant a tree?

MAYA (*leaving*). Why don't you grow some tits?

VIV. Good luck paying for the rising petrol!

MAYA. I don't pay it!

VIV. Exactly!

> MAYA *and* TRISTAN *and the group disappear into the school. The bell rings.*

I stung her like a bee.

> DANA *nods:* VIV *really didn't. They walk towards the school steps.*

Remember our mantra: today is the first day of the rest of our lives.

> DANA *smiles, but isn't too sure.*
>
> *A chair moves in next to her. Transition into –*
>
> *Admissions adviser's office. The* ADMISSIONS ADVISER *sits on a chair.* DANA *sits down on a chair opposite.*

ADMISSIONS ADVISER. Well, you are restricted by your lack of… talking. I'm guessing you'll apply for remote learning only? And then you can always do a voice–text response in tutorials online. Like Stephen Hawking.

Or *Siri.*

Thing is, Dana… You did do extremely well in your GCSEs. You've got a very strong case for applying, well, anywhere. What about University College London, or St Andrews, or *Oxbridge*?

Ah, but most of these top universities require an interview. Would you…?

*The* ADVISER *waits for an answer.* DANA *shakes her head.*

There may be a case for positive discrimination – *Malala* got accepted into Oxford after being shot by the Taliban.

DANA *stares at the* ADVISER, *her eyes nearly rolling out of her head.*

Yes, it's not a reliable parallel, but you do have an EHCP.

DANA *can't say anything. Deflated, the* ADVISER *hands her a pile of prospectuses.*

Work on your personal statement. Make your voice heard. And spellcheck, for crying out loud – you have no idea how many applications I see that leave the 'p' out of psychology.

DANA *gets up. The* ADVISER *disappears.*

DANA (*to the audience*). I can't remember the exact day I stopped speaking. Or even why. But I remember people's reactions.

They think I'm being difficult. Or shy. They don't get it. It's not a choice. It's not that I *won't* speak. I literally, physically *can't* speak. I get so anxious –

*The* COMPANY *look at her.*

My throat tightens.

*The* COMPANY *beat their feet on the floor – ba-boom, ba-boom – like a heartbeat. They move closer.* DANA *stands on a chair.*

I go hot. Palms sweat. Arms tingle.

Words get trapped in my trachea. Face freezes.

My heart beats out my chest. Everything sounds so far away.

*The* COMPANY *close in on her.*

And then I'm in the sea. Waves of panic overwhelming me. The land getting further and further away.

*The* COMPANY *are the sea – like a wave moving up and down, around her; she reaches up, trying to reach above the water.*

I try to catch a breath. But I can't. Everything's stuck.

*She tries to reach up again, and sinks below the waves.*

*Suddenly the waves part. The* COMPANY *set up a classroom around her, chairs facing towards the audience.*

I'm seventeen, and I speak to exactly the same number of people I spoke to when I was four.

One: My mum. And as you can imagine, that's a double-edged sword.

Two: Myself. Which is having a conversation with someone who gets me. Even if it's someone I don't always like.

*She sits down on a chair.*

Thing is – nobody wants to be different.

*A classroom. A* CLASSICS TEACHER *stands at the front, pointing at two (imaginary) pictures of identical vases on the board. The class look extremely bored, apart from* VIV *who is scribbling down notes.*

CLASSICS TEACHER. As you can see, these two Attic vases are vastly different. Can anyone tell me the differences between the red-figure Attic vase, and the black-figure Attic vase?

VIV*'s hand shoots up.*

Anyone else? The red-figure Attic vase… and the black-figure Attic vase…

Tom?

TOM. Erm… one is red and one is black?

CLASSICS TEACHER. Yes, anything more refined…? technique; function; composition…

DANA*'s hand nervously goes up.*

Oh, Dana Alford, this is a surprise.

DANA *takes a deep breath, a pause, and then she holds up a large card – it has a picture of a toilet on it. The class laugh.*

MAYA. Ancient hieroglyphics.

YAZ. Dana needs to go peepee.

VIV. Shut it.

TRINH. Grow up.

VIV. Your call is important to us, please stay on the line whilst no one gives a shit.

CLASSICS TEACHER (*to* DANA). I presume you can't wait. Off you go. Enough disrupting the class.

DANA*, mortified, gets up and leaves the classroom. The classroom dismantles.*

DANA (*to audience*). An Attic vase originates from the province of Ancient Athens. The black-figure vase pre-dates the red-figure vase, but they are basically the same.

DANA *walks along the school corridor.*

We pretend to celebrate difference, accommodate it. In reality, we just stick a label on it and put it in a kind of storage unit so it doesn't make the rest of the world look untidy – like my mum does with all her junk stuffed into the top drawer in the kitchen. Let me show you the Calming Room. Also known as the De-escalation Room. The junk drawer of life. Also known as –

The 'Freaks and Geeks' Room.

*A number of pupils sit on chairs or on the floor.* CON *can easily be mistaken for an adult – he's a student, and self-appointed leader.*

CON. Hey, Dana.

DANA *waves.*

Come in. Make yourself super comfortable. We were just discussing Kierkegaard's take on the frailty of the human condition. Nah, not really, Jono was burping out the hymn 'Jerusalem', but then he followed through at the end, which was fun… but messy. There's some newbies here you need to meet. So, let's check in.

DANA *finds a chair and sits.*

Okay, attention, Freaks and Geeks! Dana's in the house. Roll call, please!

*Each person says their name and disorder.*

JONO. Jono. TikTok tic.

ANITA. Anita. Pathological avoidance disorder.

TONI. Toni. Autism.

PETE. Pete. Autism.

SAINI. Saini. Autism.

CON. Con. Agoraphobia.

HOLLY. Holly. I'd rather not say.

CON. Respect.

MO. Mo. ADHD.

*They all turn to* VIV, *who's sitting on a chair.*

PETE. What the hell's she doing in here?

MO. There's nothing wrong with you.

VIV. I have generalised anxiety about the climate crisis.

SAINI. Word!

CON (*pointing at* DANA). Dana, selective mutism. Come into the bosom of our sanctuary.

PETE. Buzoom!

MO (*to* DANA). Have you started taking the drugs yet?

DANA *shakes her head.*

TONI. She wouldn't be on the same drugs as you – different disorder, different drugs.

MO. You should take the drugs. They're really good.

TONI. Knucklehead.

CON. Hey, none of that in here.

MO (*whispers*). Take the drugs.

CON. This is a safe space. Out there – in the normative world – it's chaos. You gotta start seeing the people out there as freaks.

PETE. Amen.

JONO. They speaketh the truth.

SAINI. Word!

CON. They're trying to control us with their therapies, and their Ritalin, in their 'how to be normative' world. Our difference is our safe place.

JONO. It's our superpower.

ANITA. That is one messed-up *Avengers* movie.

SAINI. Word!

HOLLY. Only –

CON (*snaps*). Only what? (*Then.*) I mean, Holly, go ahead, you have the floor.

HOLLY. Isn't the whole point that we get out of here?

CON. Excuse me?

HOLLY. We learn how to move on.

CON. And go where? Where do you want to go?

JONO. KFC.

CON. Nobody is preventing your visit to KFC.

TONI. KFC is dangerous.

VIV. Those are not happy chickens.

PETE (*re* VIV). Why's she here again?

VIV (*overlapping*). Stuffed full of steroids and antibiotics.

TONI. Once my dog ate a drumstick from KFC, bone splintered in his stomach, Mum had forgotten to renew the pet insurance. That was not a good day.

CON (*interrupting*). Okay, Everyone, *meditation*. Let's all think about this disruption.

HOLLY *stops* DANA *as she leaves.*

HOLLY (*whispers*). There's no calm room after this. No de-escalation. You get out into the real world, and there's no SENCO, there's no paediatric psychs, you're out there in the grown-up forest – and you're not like any of the other trees, you're out there, different. And alone.

MO. Take the drugs.

*The* COMPANY *chant the name of drugs. They run on with a large imaginary skipping rope, and skip into the rope, chanting the drugs, faster and faster, over and over –*

THE COMPANY. Sertraline

St John's wort

Beta blockers

Lexapro

Prozac

Zoloft

Celexa

Valium

Xanax

Klonopin

Sertraline

St John's wort

Beta blockers…

DANA *can't run into the skipping rope and join in. She tries. She freezes. The skipping and chanting stop.*

DANA. I'm not against drugs – I know they can help. But part of me feels safe with what I know. Safe in being untouched and untouchable. And part of me feels terrified.

I'm terrified of changing. And I'm terrified of staying the same.

*The school therapy room. An overearnest* THERAPIST *sits on a chair, feet planted on the floor, in perfect Alexander Technique positioning.*

THERAPIST. I'm pleased you've made it to our session this week, Dana. We're going to continue with 'Fading In'.

DANA (*to the audience*). Fading in is a kind of *exposure therapy.*

THERAPIST (*continues*). Say, for instance, if you were scared of snakes. 'Ooh… snakes are scary.' Which may seem like a completely rational fear BUT you are extremely unlikely in your lifetime to ever be harmed by a snake. *Back to fading in.* You start by sitting here, and there's a snake outside the room.

*Someone enters on the periphery holding a snake.*

In a box, of course. The snake would be in a box.

*They put the snake in a pet-carrier box.*

And you think 'There's a scary snake outside this room.' But then you slowly carry on doing what you're doing, and soon you completely forget about that snake. You realise, 'Oh, that snake's not hurting me. It's not scary. This is fine. In fact, it's so fine, that snake might be able to move a little bit closer.'

*The* COMPANY *take a step forward, and more people enter holding snakes.* DANA *watches them, as they slowly step closer and closer, encircling her, whilst the* THERAPIST *continues.*

Same with talking. You have an irrational fear of speaking. So we *fade in*. You talk with someone standing outside the room. And, look… Nothing bad has happened. You think, 'Oh there's someone outside the room, and maybe they've heard me and that's okay, I haven't *died*.' So they take a step closer –

*The* COMPANY *take a step closer.* DANA *starts to sweat.*

DANA (*to the audience*). Is it me, or is it getting very hot in here?

THERAPIST (*noticing* DANA *panicking*). You're having a little panic there. That's okay. They can take a step back –

*The* COMPANY *take a step back.*

You breathe. Everything settles. And then they keep going.

DANA (*to the audience*). This can take forever, by the way.

*The* COMPANY *step closer.*

And then…

THERAPIST. You're doing so well.

*The* COMPANY *step closer and closer, closing in on* DANA.

DANA. Like a really bad game of Grandmother's Footsteps…

THERAPIST. No point in giving up now.

DANA (*shouts*). You suddenly find there's a motherfucking snake staring right at you!

*DANA stands on a chair, her breathing is fast, she clutches her neck. Everyone disappears, apart from the* THERAPIST.

THERAPIST. So, that didn't go so well today. Let's try again next week.

*An organ plays the hymn 'Amazing Grace'. Everyone assembles on chairs in rows for assembly. The* HEADTEACHER *stands at the front, addressing the school.*

HEADTEACHER. Good morning, Stretford Grammar. Firstly, I'd like to say a hearty congratulations to our rugby team, led by captain Tristan Khan, who came top in the under-eighteens fixture. Tristan was also named 'Man of the Match'.

NAV (*shouts*). He's the man!

*Someone wolf-whistles.*

HEADTEACHER. Inappropriate!

Capitalising on our vertiginous GCSE results, we can expect a bumper crop of top university offers. We can show the North London Collegiates, the Henrietta Barnetts, the Manchester Grammars –*

*There's a big rival 'boo' from the students.*

---

* Put in your own choice of three local schools or colleges here, if you like.

Haha. Yes, indeed –

*The 'boos' get louder.*

Alright. (*Shouts.*) Quieten down! We shall be using a *buddy system* – pairing up sixth-formers, to help prepare your personal statements, and work on interview technique.

You shall be going to battle with your peers. And the importance of war is to know thine enemy. Buddy pairs will be pinned to the sixth-form noticeboard after recess.

MAYA. Hope I'm not paired up with *The Mute*.

VIV (*to* MAYA). Meathead.

MAYA. Vegan tits.

VIV. What is it with my tits today?

HEADTEACHER. Now, please stand and sing hymn number twenty-two in your hymn books.

*The organ plays 'Amazing Grace'. People stand, and sing as they clear chairs away.* DANA *stands still amidst all the movement and singing.*

STUDENTS (*singing*).
Amazing grace, how sweet the sound,
That saved a wretch like me.
I once was lost –

DANA *joins in, everyone ignores her; their voices peter out until she sings alone.*

DANA *and* STUDENTS (*singing*).
But now am found.
Was blind but now I see.

*Her voice soars, beautiful, but no one on stage hears it. A lone voice.*

DANA (*singing*).
Was blind but now I see.

*Someone stands holding a piece of paper – they are the sixth-form noticeboard. Students go up and look at the noticeboard.* VIV *approaches with* DANA; *they look at the list.* DANA's *eyes widen. She walks downstage.* VIV *follows her.*

VIV. That's really stupid – why didn't they put us together?

DANA *doesn't answer.*

Listen, I can come along. If it's difficult for you.

DANA *shakes her head. She holds up her toilet card.*

Right. Cool. Well, I'll be in the library. If you want to join me. I'm writing a letter to our local MP about fishing quotas. These fish won't save themselves. Well, they would. If they were more sentient.

Oh, and we've got to practise our moves.

VIV *dances.* DANA *joins her.*

Go fishies. Go fishies. You're actually dancing like you need the toilet.

DANA *jokingly gives* VIV *the finger. They laugh.* VIV *dances off.*

Go fishies. Go fishies.

*A row of chairs set up to be toilet cubicles. This is the girls' bathroom.* TRINH *sits in a cubicle.* DANA *sits in the cubicle next to her. The gang of* COOL GIRLS *stare into the mirror – which is the fourth wall – talking out to the audience. They don't know* DANA *is there.* DANA *can hear everything.*

MAYA. I can't believe The Mute is paired up with Tristan. (*Putting on lip balm.*) He doesn't need someone with a speech impediment helping him with interview technique. He's walking into Oxbridge on a sports scholarship.

YAZ. Oxbridge isn't a place, moron.

MAYA. Of course it is.

YAZ. It's two separate places. He can't be in two places at once.

TRINH. Guys –

LAURA. I heard The Mute's applying to Oxford.

MAYA. Like, not to be offensive, but this is going to reflect really badly on the school.

YAZ. It's inclusivity gone mad.

LAURA. She won't turn up to a meeting with him. She can barely leave home –

MAYA. I bet she does. She's obsessed with me and Tristan.

*DANA rolls her eyes, shakes her head.*

Always staring at us.

YAZ. Is she though?

MAYA. I can feel those big cow eyes boring into me.

YAZ. You think everyone's staring at you. You're a narcissist.

MAYA. All seventeen-year-olds are narcissists, but thanks for the unwarranted character assassination, bitch!

TRINH. Guys!

YAZ. He won't turn up to the meeting with her. He's got better things to do.

TRINH. Guys! There's no toilet roll.

LAURA. I heard when she was five, she was crossing the road between Joe and the Juice and Iceland. A car ran her over. It was such an enormous shock, all her hair fell out and her voice stopped working.

YAZ. I heard her dad had a heart attack right in front of her, and she tried to give him CPR, she was pumping at his chest like she was in *Holby City*, and by the time the ambulance came, he was dead. She never spoke again.

*DANA slaps her forehead.*

LAURA. Her dad's alive, you idiot.

YAZ. Joe and the Juice has only been on the high street a year!

MAYA. I heard there are these kids who don't learn how to talk. They grow up without human contact, learn how to behave from wild animals, raised by wolves, living on scraps from the bin. They stare at the moon and howl.

LAURA. I bet she walks up the hill at night and howls.

LAURA *howls. They howl like wolves.*

TRINH. Guys, I don't know what's going on out there, but there's no toilet roll!!

DANA *comes out of the cubicle. The* COOL GIRLS *look at her and stop howling.* DANA *passes some toilet roll to* TRINH *and runs off.*

*The* COMPANY *enter the stage, howling like wolves.* DANA *runs through them, running through the forest as we transition to –*

TRISTAN *waits onstage, alone, his sports bag on the floor. He looks around, sighs, checks his watch –*

*He shakes his head. He picks up his bag, and goes to exit.* DANA *walks onstage, heavy rucksack on her back.*

TRISTAN. We were supposed to meet half an hour ago.

DANA *doesn't say anything.*

I've got strength training now.

DANA *doesn't say anything.*

I wasn't gonna come, you know. And now I've gotta go.

DANA *nods. She can't look him in the eye. Frustrated,* TRISTAN *leaves.* DANA *stands alone on the stage. Alone. Again. She goes to walk off.*

TRISTAN *walks back on.*

I'm gonna get ribbed for not training with the team. That's what teams are all about: turning up.

*He puts his bag down.*

So how do we do this? How do we – [*talk*]?

*He's getting nothing back from* DANA.

This is a bit… frustrating.

DANA *pulls a phone out of her pocket. She hands it to him.*

What?

*She points to him. Then she points to the phone.*

Oh, right… what? You want me to put my Snap in here?

*She nods. He sighs. He puts his number in her contacts. He passes her back the phone.*

DANA *starts to type a Snapchat. An actor stands behind* DANA *as she types – they are playing* DANA'S MESSAGE. DANA *sends the message. There's a 'ping'.* TRISTAN *takes his phone out, and looks at it.*

DANA'S MESSAGE. We can chat. Smiley face.

TRISTAN *types. An actor –* TRISTAN'S MESSAGE *– stands behind him.* TRISTAN *sends the message.*

TRISTAN'S MESSAGE. Okay.

DANA *types.*

DANA'S MESSAGE. Sorry I was late.

TRISTAN *types.*

TRISTAN'S MESSAGE. Whatever.

TRISTAN *stops. Taps the phone.*

Delete. Delete. Delete.

TRISTAN *types.*

So what are you applying for?

DANA'S MESSAGE. English. You?

TRISTAN'S MESSAGE. Same.

DANA*'s eyes widen as she reads the message.* TRISTAN *types.*

Hey, what's with the face?

DANA'S MESSAGE. It's just my face.

TRISTAN'S MESSAGE. I got a really strong score in my GCSE English.

DANA'S MESSAGE. You want to do English at Oxford?

TRISTAN'S MESSAGE. Where are you applying?

DANA'S MESSAGE (*hesitates*). UCL. Maybe.

TRISTAN'S MESSAGE. You know you have to interview for UCL?

DANA'S MESSAGE. You know you have to interview for Oxford?

*TRISTAN looks at his phone, surprised. He stops.*

TRISTAN. I don't actually have to type. I can speak.

DANA *types.*

DANA'S MESSAGE. You shouldn't type. You spelled 'interview' wrong.

*TRISTAN looks at his phone, scrolls back through the messages.*

TRISTAN'S MESSAGE (*reading back*). 'Inter-veiw.'

TRISTAN *types.*

Smart-ass.

DANA'S MESSAGE. Arse. A-R-S-E.

*He looks at her, frustrated. He picks up his bag.*

TRISTAN. I don't need to be here –

*She waves him goodbye. He looks at her, totally perplexed and frustrated.*

So why don't you speak?

*She looks at him.*

Why – don't – you – speak?

*DANA gets out her phone, and starts typing.* TRISTAN *starts reading his phone.*

DANA'S MESSAGE. After my father dropped dead in front of my very eyes, and I failed to resuscitate him even though I have a Bronze Level Duke of Edinburgh Award, I was raised by a pack of savage wolves. They called me *White Fang Dana* –

TRISTAN. Okay –

DANA'S MESSAGE. And taught me how to hunt with my human paws, and howl at the full moon, but they did not, and could not, teach me how to speak.

*DANA has finished. She stares at him.*

TRISTAN. Okay. I get it. None of my business.

*A silence.*

Listen, do you want to swap personal statements?

*She stands there.*

If you don't want us to help each other, what are you doing here?

DANA *shrugs.*

I know why we're paired up, okay. You're a whizz at English. You're a wordsmith. And I'm a meathead. That's what you're thinking: I'm a meathead, who's going to walk the interview because I'm one of the top youth rugby players in the county. I'm the top player. But, you're right, I can't write as well as you can. So are we gonna help each other out, or what?

DANA *types.*

DANA'S MESSAGE. You think I'm a *wordsmith*?

TRISTAN. Ironically, yes.

DANA *reaches into her bag and pulls out a piece of paper – her personal statement. She hands it to* TRISTAN, *barely able to look at him.* TRISTAN *glances at the piece of paper.*

This just has one sentence on it. That's all you can think to say about yourself?

DANA *shrugs. He takes a piece of paper out of his bag and hands it to her.*

Let's meet up tomorrow and we can talk this through. Text. Whatever.

DANA *gets her phone out, and writes. A ping.* TRISTAN *looks at his phone.*

DANA'S MESSAGE. Okay.

TRISTAN *goes to leave. Another ping.*

Meathead.

*He looks at* DANA *and smiles. She smiles back. He leaves.*

*She looks down at* TRISTAN*'s personal statement. She takes a pen and starts crossing through things.* VIV *enters, holding a placard with 'Walk for the Earth' written on it.*

VIV. Hey, do you want to come to the march in town?

DANA *holds up the piece of paper she's editing.*

Right. Work. Hey, how did it go with Tristan?

DANA *pulls a face.*

Yeah, well, the dude's a meathead.

DANA *nods.*

See ya tomorrow.

VIV *leaves. But* DANA *doesn't actually think* TRISTAN *is a meathead.*

*The* COMPANY *march across the stage holding placards, they weave around* DANA. *Each shouting a slogan.*

THE COMPANY. Save the Earth.

Save the trees.

Save the forests.

Trees give life.

DANA *puts headphones on, listens to music, loudly. We hear the music she can hear; it drowns out the slogan-chanters and the* COMPANY *turn to trees in the background.*

TRISTAN *enters. He taps* DANA *on the shoulder to get her attention. She takes her headphones off, the music stops.*

TRISTAN. Hey.

DANA *waves.*

Thanks for your notes. Harsh. But fair. I would say there is a fine line between confidence and arrogance –

DANA *smiles, she takes her finger and draws an imaginary line across the ground. Then she crosses over the imaginary line.*

Okay, I may have crossed that line. It's not all arrogance –

*She looks at him.*

I've toned it down. I've even added something about English literature.

*She does a mock clap. He smiles. He hands her her personal statement.*

There wasn't much to go on here. You know you've gotta sell yourself, Dana. This is your one shot to make your mark. You're in competition with everybody else applying, except…

*He stops.* DANA *looks at him – 'What?'*

You're really clever. I looked at your results –

*She takes the piece of paper from him, embarrassed.*

You should be applying to Oxford –

DANA *shakes her head.*

So… what? You're just going to stay here? Do university online?

*She shrugs.*

The whole point of university is that you escape, you meet people, you interact, you get drunk, you throw up. You regret, you make mistakes, you get a job. You work out how to be in the real world. What's the point of all this otherwise?

*She looks at him. He stops. A silence between them. He's extremely frustrated. He looks at her headphones.*

What you listening to?

DANA *shrugs – 'Nothing much.'*

TRISTAN *puts his headphones on. He gestures to her phone.*

Can I – ?

*She hesitates, then hands him her phone. He goes to her music, presses play. Rocks his head around. We don't hear it – just* TRISTAN *does, through the headphones.*

Okay. Good choice. Angry.

*He starts singing the song she's listening to – 'You Oughta Know' by Alanis Morissette.*

(*Shouts to* DANA.) What? I can't hear you? You're gonna have to speak louder.

*Of course, she's not saying anything. She can't help smiling.*

I've got an idea. You rock out, right? You put your music on loud. I bet you scream, right? Shout it out loud, like nobody's watching?

*He puts her headphones over her ears. She looks at him, perplexed.*

You can't hear me with the music playing –

*He puts his headphones on.*

And I can't hear you.

*He whacks the music up loud. He can hear it.* DANA *can hear it. The song fills the auditorium. He smiles at* DANA, *and starts screaming along to it. He gets into it, headbangs.* DANA *watches him.*

TRISTAN *sings the chorus, then totally commits to the verse, getting some words wrong –*

DANA *closes her eyes; she starts to sing and shout along with him.*

TRISTAN *looks at her. He takes off his headphones. He watches her singing, aloud, her eyes shut.*

DANA *opens her eyes; she sees* TRISTAN *watching her, headphones off. She covers her mouth, shocked.*

Dana –

*She grabs her stuff.*

Nothing bad happened!

*She runs off through the forest.*

Dana!

*The Freaks and Geeks Room* – CON *is leading the usual suspects in a yoga class. They are all in various, individual states of the tree pose.*

CON. And hands raised above and open – like the growing fruit trees of life –

MO. Fruit cakes, more like.

CON. Trees do not talk.

And… breathe.

DANA *runs in.*

Hey, Dana. We're doing yoga practice. Would you like to adopt the tree pose?

PETE. You'll be good at this. Trees don't talk.

SAINI. Word.

DANA *sits down, her heart is thumping in her chest. Her breathing is shallow.* CON *looks at her.*

CON. Shallow breath?

*She nods.*

SAINI. Heart racing?

ANITA. Tingling arms?

TONI. Jelly legs?

JONO. Sweaty palms?

*She nods.*

MO. Panic attack!

CON. Stand back, everyone.

Okay, Dana, look at me. Look into my eyes. Focus. Focus. Regulate your breathing. Breathe in and out.

*She shakes her head. She can't.*

Yes, you can.

MO. You can do it, Dana.

PETE. You can do it.

HOLLY. Shouldn't we call a nurse?

CON. No! What happens in Freaks and Geeks, stays in Freaks and Geeks. (*To* DANA.) Look at me –

*They breathe with her, in and out –*

In and out. In and out. You're a tree.

You're a beautiful, individual tree.

DANA (*to the audience*). I don't want to be an individual tree. I want to connect. I want to be able to laugh and love, and be loved back. I want to be able to go to crowded places. And ask for a coffee in Starbucks. And tell my grandma I love her before she croaks. And ask for directions when I'm lost in a dark wood. I want to go to parties, and drink, and throw up –

I want to be able to speak, without throwing up.

CON. That's it. She's good. Nothing to see here, folks. Back to downward dog.

*They get back to downward dog. As others set up chairs around them.*

And into Sun salutation. Salute the Sun.

MO. Hello Sun!

STUDENT 1. Shhhh.

*Someone shushes them. The Freaks and Geeks Room breaks up. We're in the school library.*

STUDENT 2. Shhhh.    STUDENT 3. Shhhh.

*The* COMPANY *'shushes' as they sit on chairs, reading books.* DANA *sits on a chair in the library, tapping on a computer. The character of* DANA'S WORD DOC *stands behind the computer, speaking the words* DANA *is typing.*

DANA'S WORD DOC. My name is Dana Alford, this is my personal state–

DANA *tap. Tap. Taps.*

Delete. Delete. Delete.

DANA *types.*

My personal heroes are Maya Angelou, Ruth Bader Ginsberg, and Little Red Riding Hood – who far from being a victim, was a survivor of parental neglect.

DANA, *frustrated, presses hard on a button.*

Del-e-e-e-e-e-e-e-e-e-e-e-e-e-e-e-te.

DANA (*to audience*). I've got to make myself stand out, even though I'm already different to everyone else. But I'm not the right kind of different –

TRISTAN. Dana –

STUDENT 3. Shhhh –

TRISTAN *walks into the library and sits on the chair next to her.* DANA *keeps typing, ignores him.*

TRISTAN. Hello?

DANA *tries to ignore him, and continues to type.*

So I heard your voice. That's a good thing, isn't it? If you can talk to me, you can maybe even talk in an interview. Can you stop typing, it's actually quite rude –

*She stops, stares daggers at him, and packs up to leave.*

Don't leave.

STUDENT 1. Shhhh.

DANA *types on to the computer.*

DANA'S WORD DOC. You tricked me into talking –

TRISTAN. Isn't that what the therapy is? Getting into uni. Being popular. Successful. Surviving this world is one big trick. You want to talk, right?

*She gets up.*

Dana, wait!

STUDENT 2. Shhhhh.

STUDENT 3. Quiet!

DANA *goes to leave.*

TRISTAN. My mum cleans offices in the Southfield industrial estate. My dad hasn't worked for nearly ten years. I am going to be the first person in my family to go to university. They have huge expectations of me to be a success. Be the best. And I have to be grateful for the opportunities they never had, even though –

STUDENT 4. Shhhh!   STUDENT 1. Shhhh!

TRISTAN. Sometimes I can't be bothered to go training at seven in the morning –

*She stops for a second. Listens to him.*

(*Continues.*) I don't want to stand there in the sleet and the mud and have posh boys the size of my dad hurl themselves at me. Sometimes I just want to lie in, and see no one, and order pizza, and watch YouTube. And I know you know how it must feel to try for something, and think you've already failed –

DANA *sits on the chair, and types on the computer.* TRISTAN *reads the screen.*

DANA'S WORD DOC. No one expects anything of me.

TRISTAN. That's not true.

STUDENT 2. Shhh!

TRISTAN (*angrily, to* STUDENT 2). What's your problem?

STUDENT 2. It's a library – that's my problem.

TRISTAN. You know that's not true, Dana!

STUDENT 1. Shhhh!

TRISTAN (*shouts*). I said, stop shushing me!

STUDENT 4. Quieten down!

TRISTAN (*screams*). Ahhhhhhhhhh!

DANA *looks at him – 'What are you doing?'*

I'm doing exactly what people aren't expecting. Ahhhhhhhhhhh!

LIBRARIAN. Stop it, or you'll have to be removed!

TRISTAN *runs between the chairs of seated people.*

TRISTAN. Come on. I swear, it feels great! Ahhhhhhhhhhhhhh!

*She hesitates, then –*

DANA. Ahhhhhhhhhhhhhhhh!

*He stands on a chair.*

TRISTAN. Ahhhhhhhh! That's it!

*She gets on a chair.*

DANA (*howls*). Ah-wooooooo.

TRISTAN. Ah-wooooo!

*All the* STUDENTS *howl.*

VIV *walks in and sees* DANA *howling with* TRISTAN. *The* HEADTEACHER *walks in. Everyone stops howling.* DANA *and* TRISTAN *stop howling.*

HEADTEACHER. Tristan, I expected better of you! Detention!

Dana – erm, well… this is… complex… Let me think about this.

VIV *looks at* DANA, *hurt.* VIV *runs off.*

DANA *stays on her chair. The rest of the* COMPANY *surround her, moving in closer… closer.*

DANA (*to the audience*). My heart's thumping, like it's in my throat. My mouth's dry. The adrenalin rising. Body's in fight or flight. Everything goes quiet, and far away –

*The* COMPANY *are waves surrounding her.*

The waves come. But somehow I stay above water. I gasp for air, and it goes in. Past my throat, and into my lungs. I watch the people on the shore, as I try to find my footing out at sea, but they're not looking. I thought they'd be staring.

*She reaches up to wave above the water.*

I'm waving, but I'm not drowning. 'Dana spoke… who gives a crap?'

But to me, it's a tsunami of epic proportions.

*Loud music.* DANA *jumps down from the chair into the human wave. The wave disperses.* DANA *stands there watching* VIV, *who is practising recording her TikTok dance on her phone, which is propped up on a chair.*

*She ignores* DANA, *and does the dance defiantly on her own.* VIV *mucks up the steps. She goes back, deletes it on her phone. Presses record again. Tries again, even more defiantly.*

VIV. You just gonna stand there and watch?

DANA *doesn't say anything.*

What's the matter – cat got your tongue?

DANA *doesn't say anything.* VIV *turns her back on her, and dances defiantly to her phone's camera. She stops.*

Why wasn't it me?

DANA *doesn't speak.*

I've done my homework on your condition. I read the books. I tried to do *fading in* with you. I stuck by you, when everyone else was laughing behind our backs.

Why was it Tristan you spoke to first? Why wasn't it me?

DANA *can't speak. She starts texting on her phone.*

I know, I'm *contaminated*, right? Someone you've got a history of not speaking to. So instead you choose the male saviour? I mean, holy crap, Dana… have you been reading too much Jane Austen, or what?

*There's a text-message ping.* VIV *picks up her phone and reads.*

DANA TEXT MESSAGE. It means so much to you –

VIV. Of course it does.

DANA TEXT MESSAGE. That's not a question. I know it does. I want to talk so badly, but I don't want to let you down. I don't want to let anyone I care about down. It makes me... paralysed.

VIV. So now it's my fault?

*A silence.* DANA *types on her phone.*

DANA TEXT MESSAGE. I guess I spoke to Tristan because I don't care about him. I care about disappointing you.

VIV *is silent. After a moment,* VIV *pulls the sleeve of her T-shirt down – her shoulder has a giant plaster on it.*

DANA *looks at her – 'What happened?'*

VIV *peels the plaster back – we don't necessarily have to see what's underneath.* DANA *looks at* VIV, *shocked.*

VIV. It's Greta Thunberg.

DANA *types. Ping.*

DANA TEXT MESSAGE. W... T... A... F.

VIV. It'll look more like Greta Thunberg when it heals. Right now, it looks like Boris Johnson.

DANA *looks at her – 'Why?'*

Okay, firstly, Greta Thunberg is a legend. Secondly, she didn't speak. She stopped speaking when she was a kid, for years. She had what you have. And people called her 'shy', and 'difficult', and 'angry'. But she wasn't. She was terrified. And she was in pain. And she took all of that, and she turned it into her superpower. Greta Thunberg is a superhero, Dana.

That's why I did this.

VIV *gestures to her shoulder.*

Because it was painful – don't believe what anyone tells you, it really really hurt. Like, I had to tell the guy to stop about two hundred times. And I just wanted to feel that pain that she went through. That you go through, all the time.

*There's a long silence between them.*

DANA *puts her phone down where* VIV*'s phone was. She stands back, and dances* VIV*'s TikTok dance moves from earlier. She stops, tries to remember what* VIV *was doing, dances again.*

Nah, it was like this –

VIV *shows her the dance move.*

DANA *copies the dance move.*

Yeah, that's it.

*Music rises. They do the dance together.*

*The girls' bathroom. The* COOL GIRLS *are in a fluster.*

YAZ. Did you hear? The Mute spoke to Tristan.

MAYA. I told you she was obsessed.

LAURA. What did she say.

YAZ. She howled at him.

LAURA. I knew it.

YAZ. Not sure we can call her The Mute any more.

LAURA. What do we call her?

YAZ. Let's call her 'The Wolf'.

MAYA. That sounds way too cool.

LAURA. How about 'Diana', Goddess of the Moon? She howls at night.

YAZ. Get you, and your classical references.

LAURA. She still isn't speaking. So you don't have to worry about her seducing Tristan.

MAYA. I'm not worried.

YAZ. Yeah, apparently the freak freaked herself out.

MAYA. Why do you think I'd be worried?

LAURA. She's gone even quieter than before.

MAYA. I'm not worried.

TRINH. Maybe us talking about it isn't helping?

*They turn and stare at* TRINH *for a second or two. Chairs start to move…*

MAYA. Why haven't you done your UCAS form?

TRINH. I'm weighing up my options.

LAURA. What options?

YAZ (*leaving*). Oh my god, what did you do to your hair?

LAURA (*panics*). Nothing. Why?

YAZ. Looks blue.

LAURA. I used a hair mask.

LAURA *touches her hair as the girls exit. The location has morphed to the Freaks and Geeks Room.*

CON *is holding court, the other regulars listen attentively. It's Personal Statement Day.*

CON. This is it. This is the day to press 'send' on the rest of your life.

Or not.

Soldiers of Difference, it is time to stand up –

*They stand.*

And bear arms.

*They put their arms in the air in the 'tree position'.*

Pick up those yoga mats, and be that free, standing-alone tree in the forest of life.

TONI. Trees can't really be free – they have roots.

CON (*interrupting*). Say 'no' to getting on that A-level, university, low-paid-entry-job treadmill of Western

Civilisation. Because suddenly you may find yourself living in a shotgun shack. And you may find yourself in another part of the world. And you may find yourself behind the wheel of a large automobile. And you may find yourself in a beautiful house. With a beautiful partner. And you may ask yourself, 'Well, how did I get here?'

SAINI. Word.

MO. That's a song.

CON. What?

MO. What you just said: it's a song.

CON. No, it's not.

MO. My parents listen to that song.

CON. Coincidence.

PETE. Thing is, I do sort of want all of that.

*CON stares at PETE. Beat.*

CON. Did you do it? Did you write your personal statement like *the man* told you to? Did you toe the line?

PETE (*hesitates*). I did.

CON. Did you use adverbs, and metaphors, and the word 'plethora'?

PETE (*ashamed*). Twice.

CON. It's not your fault. You've been brainwashed by the normative world.

PETE. I haven't been brainwashed. I have an inherited condition.

CON. Don't let it define you.

HOLLY. I say, 'Let it define you!'

MO (*holding up phone*). It's a song by Talking Heads.

*They stare at CON.*

SAINI. Word.

*A few* STUDENTS *get up and start to leave.*

CON. Where are you going?

HOLLY. We've got to present our personal statements.

*Some others get up.*

CON. We're safer in numbers.

ANITA. We still have to work out how to be part of the world.

HOLLY. In order for them to accept us, we need to accept ourselves. We have to learn to live with who we are.

*JONO gets up.*

CON. Et tu, Jono?

JONO. That's from *Julius Caesar*.

TONI. You gotta attribute your citations, dude.

SAINI. Word.

*The classroom. The COMPANY sit. The HEADTEACHER addresses the class.*

HEADTEACHER. This is the first day of the rest of your lives. The day you press send on your university applications. And I would like to invite anybody sitting here, to stand and share their personal statement.

Who'd like to volunteer to go first?

*Everyone looks away, no one wants to volunteer.*

Anyone?

*TRISTAN stands holding a piece of paper. DANA stands almost immediately at the same time. The whole CLASS stare at her.*

Oh, Dana. Do you need the toilet?

*DANA shakes her head. TRISTAN nods at DANA and he sits down.*

*Everyone stares. DANA holds up her personal statement. She takes a deep breath. She goes to read it. Her mouth dries. She rubs her lips together.*

TOM. Mute!

TRISTAN. Shut up!

YAZ. Who's your boyfriend?

*The* CLASS *laugh.* MAYA *looks furious.* VIV *smiles at* DANA.

HEADTEACHER. Let her speak.

TRISTAN. Come on, Dana.

DANA *looks at the class. There's a hiss. Someone else hisses.*

VIV *gets up.*

VIV. I can do it for you. If you like?

VIV *takes the piece of paper from* DANA.

(*Reading.*) My name is Dana Alford. I'm seventeen years old. I could tell you about myself in five hundred and fifty words – my hobbies, the books I've read, where I see myself in ten years' time. But those words wouldn't actually tell you who I am –

NAV. Yawn-fest!   SAM *yawns ostentatiously.*

VIV (*continues reading*). Over my relatively short life, I've come to realise the way we communicate isn't just about words. It's not just sounds and images –

TOM (*coughs*). Bullfrogs!

VIV (*continues*). There are things –

DANA *stands and joins in.*

VIV.…we don't see or hear.   DANA. There are things we don't see or hear.

VIV *stops. Everyone stares at* DANA. *A silence.* VIV *hands* DANA *her piece of paper.* DANA *takes a deep breath and reads on, addressing the class.*

DANA. In a forest, underneath the soil, trees speak to one another. A network of fungi grow underground around their roots. This fungal network is called the Wood Wide Web –

TOM. Loser.

TRISTAN. I'm warning you –

DANA. This is all true, I saw it on a David Attenborough documentary.

VIV. David Attenborough: legend!

DANA. The trees send messages to other trees through this underground network of connected mushrooms. If they're attacked by predators, they send messages through their roots to warn neighbouring trees. They can share food or nutrients if other trees are hungry or need help. And I believe we can live in a world where human beings are like this too.

We're not in competition with each other for space and light and likes and followers and university places. We're connected in lots of other ways. We can understand each other, without always having to speak.

And lastly I've come to the conclusion that falling down is okay. John Locke was wrong: we're not just solitary trees falling down in a wood with no one hearing. Someone will hear you. Someone will catch you.

They may even join you down there on the forest floor, listening to other trees beneath the ground.

*LAURA stands.*

LAURA. I pull my hair out. I started twirling it around and around my fingers when I get worried, and now I claw at it. I rip out chunks in my sleep. I have a bald patch underneath.

SAM (*standing*). I bite my nails. Right down to the cuticle. I don't know why. They started to bleed. So I moved on to my toenails. Now I have a foot infection. I'm on antibiotics.

TRINH. I eat my feelings. I have a lot of feelings.

MAYA. I don't eat because I have no feelings.

NAV. I have these thoughts I can't get out my head. Intruding on my brain. They tell me awful stuff. I can't make them go away.

YAZ. I don't have anything wrong with me, and that makes me feel left out. So I pretend that I do.

*YAZ gets upset with her confession. People go up to YAZ to comfort her ('Hey', 'That's okay…').*

MO. I think we're gonna need a bigger Freaks and Geeks Room.

*TRINH talks to the COOL GIRLS as chairs are put into rows.*

TRINH. I'm not applying to uni.

LAURA (*shocked*). What?!

TRINH. Uni's not the be-all and end-all –

MAYA. It's the be-all and end-all.

YAZ. What are you gonna do?

TRINH. I'm gonna be an electrician's apprentice.

*TRINH pulls a light bulb out of her pocket.*

I want to make light happen.

*TRINH clicks her fingers and there's a flash of lights, like photographs being taken… school graduation.*

*The COMPANY mill around wearing mortarboards after the graduation ceremony. DANA stands around, in mortarboard, smiling and waving to people.*

TRISTAN. Hey, Dana, congrats.

*She smiles.*

DANA. Thanks. I'm sorry you didn't [*get in*] –

TRISTAN. Don't be. It's all good. I might come visit. See how the other half live.

*She nods. TRISTAN smiles. There's a silence between them. No words, but an understanding. He leaves.*

*VIV approaches, wearing a mortarboard.*

VIV. So, you know I've been totally chill about you talking and all that? I was told, back in Year 7, if you ever did speak to me, I was to put on my cool hat and just act like it was totally normal. Like, not draw attention to it.

So, I've been wearing this cool hat – you see how cool I am?

*She shows off her uncool mortarboard.*

Yeah, well, screw the hat –

VIV *flings the hat off her head and starts dancing like a maniac.*

Am I drawing attention? Are you embarrassed right now?

DANA *laughs. She dances goofily alongside* VIV.

Oh, yes, that's it. Take it to the bus station. Go Dana. Go Dana.

*They stop.*

DANA. Thanks for being the best of best friends.

VIV. Leeds is a hundred and seventy miles from Oxford. You have shorter terms than me –

DANA. I'll come visit.

VIV. You'll be okay, won't you?

DANA. Fo sho. I'll call you. If I'm not.

VIV. For what it's worth – you have an amazing voice.

*DANA smiles. The* COMPANY *flood the stage around her.*

*DANA stands on a chair.*

DANA. My name is Dana Alford – and I have a voice.

*Music swells. The* CLASS *encircle her, like before, except…*

*DANA falls backward off the chair, like a tree falling in the forest; the other people in the class are there to catch her.*

*Black.*

*The End.*

www.nickhernbooks.co.uk

facebook.com/nickhernbooks

twitter.com/nickhernbooks